Social Skills
Cooperative Play and Learning

Mini-Books to Teach Essential Social Skills

Carson Dellosa Education
Greensboro, North Carolina

Credits

Author: Christine Schwab
Illustrations: Pam Thayer, Julie Kinlaw, Erik Huffine, J.J. Rudisill

Key Education®
An imprint of Carson Dellosa Education
PO Box 35665
Greensboro, NC 27425 USA
carsondellosa.com

ISBN 978-1-4838-5693-3
01-335197784

Table of Contents

Introduction

Social skills are important. They are like good manners. Using them properly makes it easier to relate to other people with positive outcomes. Children with age-appropriate social skills can more effectively communicate, make decisions, solve problems, create and maintain successful relationships, and manage their own behavior. A lack of age-appropriate social skills interferes with children's relationships with other children, their teachers, and their family members.

Social skills do not come naturally to all children. But, social skills can be shaped. Social narratives—short stories that focus on specific social skills or desired behaviors—are useful tools to this end. They can be written or modified to meet any specific challenge.

Ideas for Using the Materials in This Book

Making the Mini-Books

This book focuses on tasks that are important in building essential skills. These pages present 13 mini-books that highlight and reinforce common behavior expectations. The illustrations are simple and printed in black and white so that children can color them. This interactive component helps children make the mini-books "their own" books.

The story pages are perforated and can be reproduced (two-sided) or assembled as single copies. Some children can cut apart and assemble the pages themselves, then staple the pages together on the left side of the books. (Check that the pages are in the correct order and help children if needed.) You may also choose to bind the books by using a hole punch and yarn or small metal rings.

Once the books are assembled, have children read their completed social narratives aloud. If a child cannot read independently, read the lines to the child. Following the first reading, have children "sign" their title pages and color the illustrations with crayons or markers. Reread the stories as needed. Over time, the narratives will become more familiar.

Repetition

New behaviors become more deeply ingrained each time they are practiced, so it is important to encourage children to read and reread their social narratives (aloud to another person). A goal chart is printed on the back page of each story to help children keep track of their progress toward a goal of reading the social story 10 times. The book concludes with award certificates for achievement and effort.

In This Book

Each mini-book in this book focuses on an important developmental social skill. They can be used in any order and as frequently as needed.

These social narratives are written in simple language so that they can be easily understood and assimilated. We hope they will prove to be an invaluable tool in shaping children's behavior.

When I Am Working in a Group

by ______________________________

When I work with a group, it is like being on a sports team. We all have to work together.

3

2

Sometimes my teacher asks me to work with other kids.
This is called group work.
A group I have worked with is ______________________.

When I work with other kids, it is important to take turns talking.
Sometimes I will sit quietly and listen.
Sometimes I will talk.

4

It is important to stay on task.
I will not talk about my favorite thing, ______________________.
I will not talk about where I am going after school.

5

I am happy when I can work in groups.
We will all learn together.

7

6 If I do not understand what the group is doing, I will ask the teacher to explain.
Or, I will ask someone in my group to explain.

I will work on meeting my goal - 10 ✔'s!

Make a ✔ each time you read your story.

On the Playground

by ______________________________

On the playground, I can swing and climb and slide.

3

2

It is fun to play on the playground.
There are a lot of kids to play with.

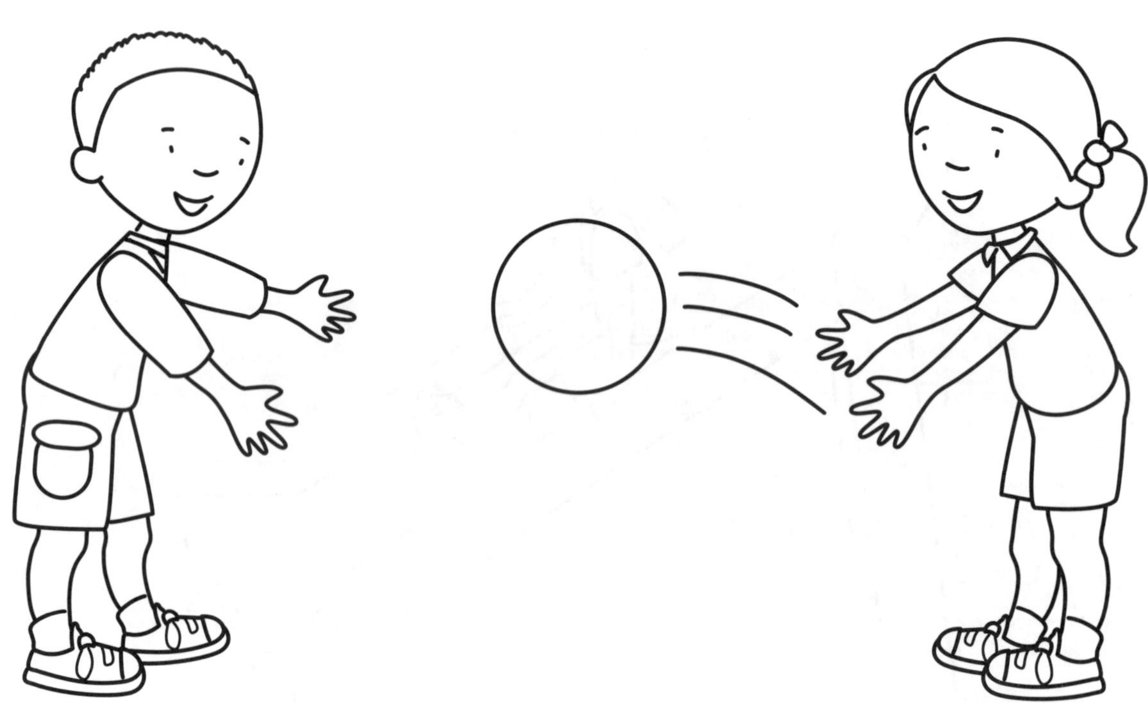

I can play ball.
I can play games with my friends.

My school has rules about playing on the playground.
I will try to follow the rules.

5

When I follow the rules, I will be safe.
My friends will want to play with me.
My teacher will be happy.

6 I will keep my hands and feet to myself.
I will listen to the playground teacher.

I will work on meeting
my goal - 10 ✔'s!

Make a ✔ each time you read your story.

I Can Make Friends

by ______________________________

There are a lot of kids to play with.
When I want to play with another person, I can walk over and ask the person to play with me.

3

2

A friend is someone I like to talk to.
A friend is someone I can play with.
I want to have friends at school.

4

I can look straight at the person's eyes and speak out loud.

I can say, "Hi, my name is ________________________. What is your name?"
Then, I can ask my new friend to play with me.

5

I like to play with other kids.
It is nice to have friends at school.
One of my friends is named ________________________.

7

6 If the person says, "No," I will say, "OK" and walk away.
If the person says, "Yes," we can play together.

I will work on meeting my goal - 10 ✔'s!

Make a ✔ each time you read your story.

When Someone Does Not Want to Play with Me

by ______________________________

Sometimes when I ask other kids to play with me, they might say, "No."

3

2 I like to play with other kids.
It makes me feel good to have friends.

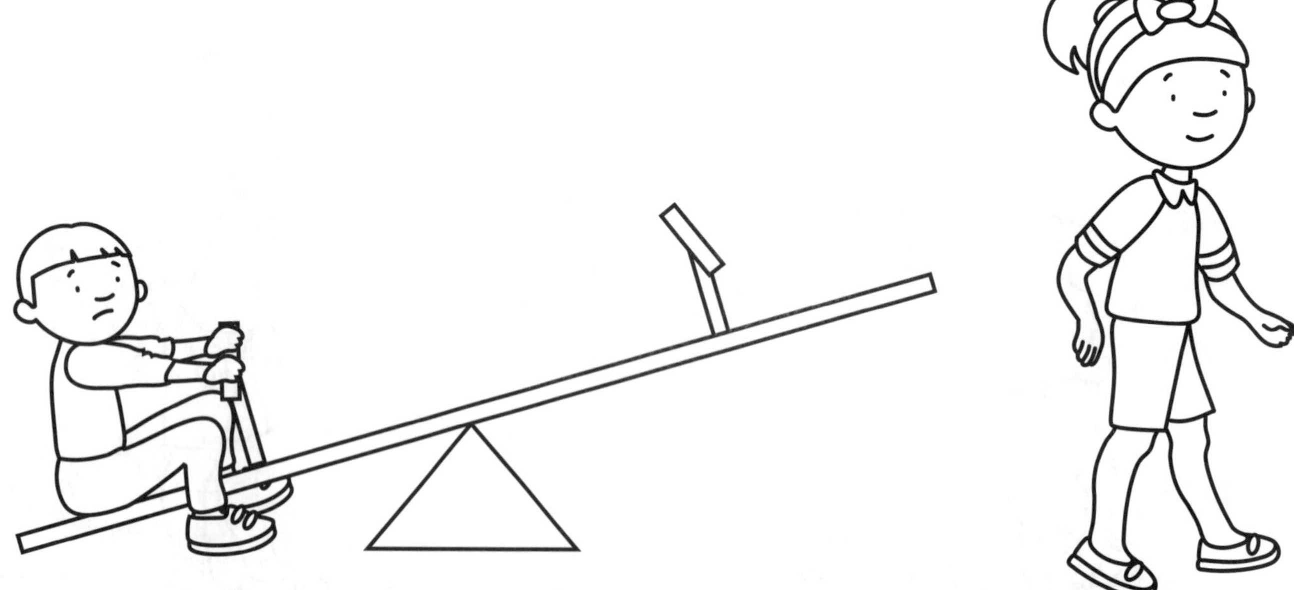

It makes me sad when other kids do not want to play with me.
But, there are many reasons my friends might not want to play with me today.

4

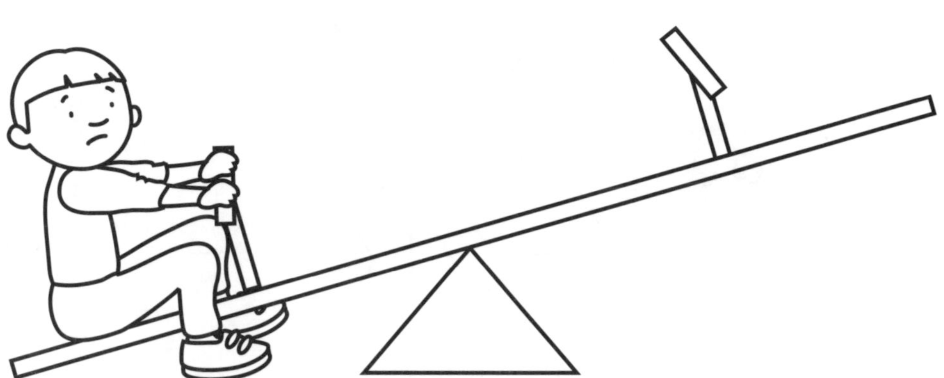

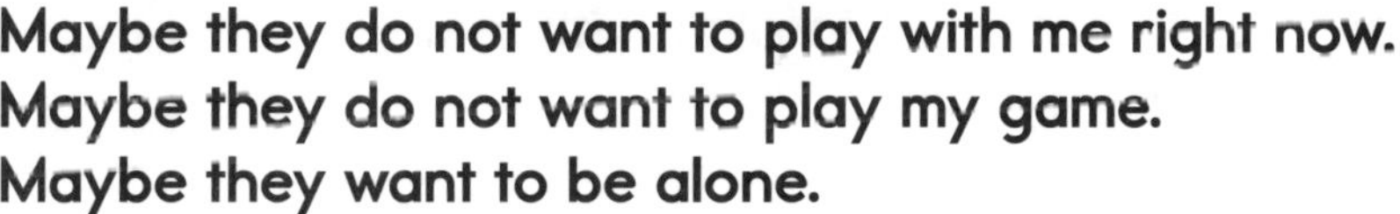

Maybe they do not want to play with me right now.
Maybe they do not want to play my game.
Maybe they want to be alone.

5

I can ask another kid to play with me. Or, I can play by myself.
I am happy when I can play games with other kids or by myself.

7

6

It is OK when other kids do not want to play with me.
It will hurt my feelings for a little bit.
Then, I will feel better.

I will work on meeting my goal - 10 ✔'s!

Make a ✔ each time you read your story.

Playing Fair

by ______________________________

I like to play games with my friends.
I will do my best to play fair.

3

2 It is a good idea to play fair with my friends.
Playing fair means treating everyone the same.
Playing fair also means playing by the rules.

4 When I play fair, I follow the rules of the game we are playing.

I will take turns with my friends.
I will try to enjoy the game whether I win or lose.

5

When I play fair, my friends like to play with me.
They will want to play with me again.

7

6 I will try to play fair.
I will not cheat or play tricks on my friends.

I will work on meeting
my goal - 10 ✔'s!

Make a ✔ each time you read your story.

Being on a Team

by ______________________________

A team is a group of kids who play a game together.
They are on the same side and try to win a game together.

3

2

I like to play games with other kids.
Some games are played by one team against another team.

I like to play on teams for games like baseball, or dodge ball,
or ________________________, my favorite.

4

When I am on a team, I will remember that I must take turns with the other kids on my team. 5

When I am a good sport and follow the rules, other kids will want me on their team.
I feel good when my friends want me on their team. 7

6 I will try to remember that I do not get to bat or kick or throw every time.
I will try to be a good sport and wait quietly until it is my turn.

I will work on meeting my goal - 10 ✔'s!

Make a ✔ each time you read your story.

When I Do Not Win

by ___________________________

I will try to remember that it is OK if I do not win.
I know that I cannot win every game.
I know that I did my best.

3

2 When kids play games, usually only one person wins.
Sometimes I will win. Sometimes I will lose.

When I do not win, I will try to be a good sport.
A good sport is polite no matter who wins the game.

4

I will try to keep on my happy face.
I will not cry or have an outburst.

5

When I am a good sport, my friends will want to play with me again.
I like to play with my friends.

7

6 If I can, I will smile at the winner.
I will try to say something like, "Good game!"

I will work on meeting my goal - 10 ✔'s!

Make a ✔ each time you read your story.

Saying "I'm Sorry"

by ______________________________

I might say something mean.
I might be rude or disrespectful.

3

2 Sometimes I do something or say something that hurts another person's feelings.

4 Other people are sad when I am mean or rude or disrespectful to them.

If I hurt someone's feelings, I will try to remember to say, "I'm sorry." 5

When I say, "I'm sorry," my friends will feel better.
I will feel better too.
It is always good to be kind to my friends. 7

6 I will say, "I'm sorry I hurt your feelings" or "I'm sorry I made you feel bad."

I will work on meeting my goal - 10 ✔'s!

Make a ✔ each time you read your story.

When Friends Disagree

by ______________________________

**But, we do not always agree.
Sometimes we like different things.
We might argue with each other.**

3

2 Sometimes my friends and I agree on almost everything.
We like the same toys. We want to play the same games.

My friend might want to play a game that I do not like.
Or, my friend might say something I do not agree with.

4

It is OK for friends to disagree.
I will try to be friendly and polite even when I do not agree.

5

My friends are happy to be with me when I am friendly and polite.
I am glad that I have friends.

7

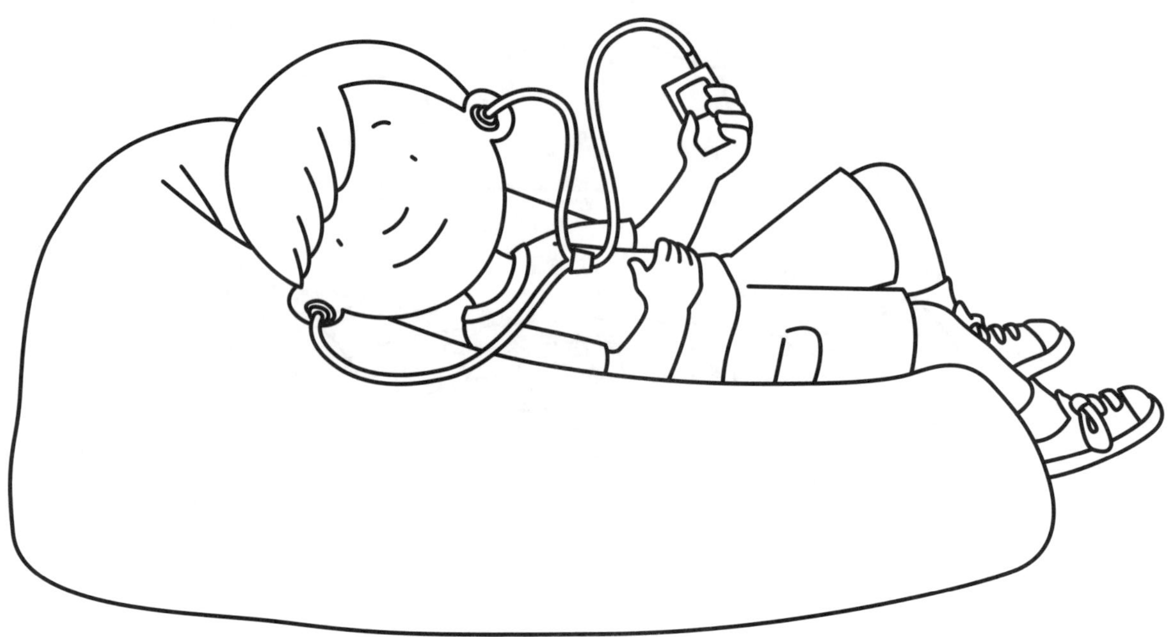

6 If I feel angry or if I want to yell at my friend, I will tell my friend that I need a break.

I will work on meeting my goal - 10 ✔'s!

Make a ✔ each time you read your story.

Playing Board Games

by ______________________________

It is important to take turns when I play board games.
That is how board games are played.
Everyone takes turns.

3

2 Sometimes I play board games with my friends.
My favorite board game is ______________________.

When it is not my turn, I will wait while my friends take their turns.
4 I will sit quietly with my hands in my lap.

At the end of the game, someone wins and someone loses.
When I am the winner, I feel happy.

5

Everyone likes to play games with a good sport.
I am proud of myself when I am a good sport.

6 When I lose the game, I will be a good sport.
I will say "Congratulations!" or "Good game!" to the winner.

I will work on meeting my goal - 10 ✔'s!

Make a ✔ each time you read your story.

Pick Me for Your Team!

by ______________________________

There are two teams for some of the games I play.
These are games like baseball, kickball,
and ____________________.

3

2

I often play games with my friends.
Sometimes I play games at school.

The captions or a teacher pick the teams.
I wonder who will pick me.

4

It makes me feel nervous when I wait to be picked for a team.
I worry that I will be the last kid to be picked. 5

I know that someone is always the last one to be picked.
When I am picked last, I will be a good sport.
I will do my best to play a good game. 7

6 Sometimes, I will be the last one to be picked.
Even if this makes me feel bad, I will join my team.

I will work on meeting my goal - 10 ✔'s!

Make a ✔ each time you read your story.

Taking Turns

by ________________________________

Everybody wants to go first.
But, not everyone can go first every time, and that includes me.

3

2

I like to play games with other kids.
When we play games, it is fun to see who goes first.

Sometimes I get to go first.
Sometimes I do not get to go first.

4

When I do not get to go first, I might feel angry or upset.

5

When I feel angry or upset, I can practice my deep breathing.
Or, I can close my eyes and count to 10.

7

6 It is okay to feel angry or upset.
But, I will try to remember that I do not have to act angry or upset.

8 I can think about all the times I got to go first in other games.

It is important for me to sit quietly.
I will try to be a good sport about not going first.

9

I am happy when I am a good sport.
My teacher is proud of me when I am a good sport.
My family is proud of me when I am a good sport.

11

(10) Other kids like playing games with me because I am such a good sport.

I will work on meeting
my goal - 10 ✔'s!

Make a ✔ each time you read your story.

Sharing My Things

by ______________________________

I do not always want to share my toys.
Sometimes I want to keep them for myself.

3

2 Sometimes it is hard to share my toys.
Sometimes I do not want to share my ______________________.

I will try to remember that I have a lot of toys to play with.
4 One toy I really like is my ______________________.

I have toys at home.
I have toys at school.

5

If someone asks to play with my toy, I will think about it.

7

6 Some of the toys are mine.
Some of the toys belong to someone else.

We can pass it back and forth.
Then, each of us can play.

8

I can let my friend play with the toy.
Then, I can find a new toy to play with.

9

It is good to share my toys, even if it is hard to do sometimes.
My friends are happy when I share my toys.
I like to have friends.

11

10 Or, if I am not finished playing with the toy, I can ask my friend to come back later.

I will work on meeting my goal - 10 ✔'s!

Make a ✔ each time you read your story.

Hooray!

____
Name

has learned how to share, take turns, and cooperate with others.

_______________________ _______________________
Signed Date

SOMETHING TO SMILE ABOUT!

____
Name

has learned how to share, take turns, and cooperate with others.

______________________ ______________________
Signed Date

by______________________________

I will work on meeting my goal - 10 ✔'s!

Make a ✔ each time you read your story.
